# CROSBY IN CAMERA

## EARLY PHOTOGRAPHS
## OF
## GREAT CROSBY & WATERLOO

Jennifer E. Stanistreet & Andrew Farthing

**SEFTON**
*LIBRARIES*

1995
Published by:
Sefton Council,
Leisure Services Department (Libraries),
Pavilion Buildings, 99-105 Lord Street
Southport PR8 1RH

Text © Jennifer E. Stanistreet & Andrew N. Farthing

Illustrations © Sefton Libraries
Care has been taken to ensure that
the reproduction of these photographs
does not infringe copyright regulations

ISBN 1-874516-07-3

Printed in Great Britain
by
Mitchell & Wright (Printers) Ltd., Southport

# INTRODUCTION

This album contains fifty early pictures of Great Crosby and Waterloo. The scenes are almost exclusively of the local communities before they were amalgamated into Crosby Borough in 1937.

The selection has been made from the extensive local history collection at Crosby Library. The emphasis is on photographs - important visual records of life as it was; the use of prints has been kept to a minimum. The breadth of Crosby's photographic collection owes much to the dedication and expertise of former librarians and local historians. Also the generosity of residents (including members of the Crosby & District Historical Society), the 'Crosby Herald' and expatriates, has enriched the collection with postcards, family snaps, topical scenes and local views. The collection, built up over many years, continues to grow - it is a storehouse of Crosby's visual history.

Inevitably, however, many aspects of life do not figure in this album. The physical condition of some photographs has prevented reproduction; and the library's collection lacks photographs of certain local buildings, events and personalities. Nonetheless, what follows may serve for many people as an introduction to the area's recent history: for others it will be a reminder of times past.

In order to assist readers in locating the site or viewpoint of the photographs, a map (centre pages) shows the district in the early years of the 20th century. A select bibliography and a full list of the photographs can be found at the back of the book.

JES/ANF
January 1995

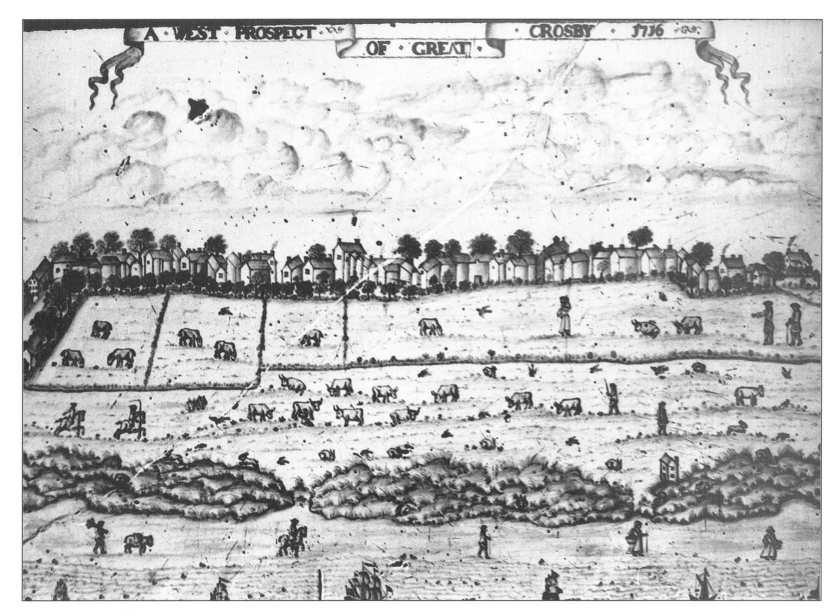

**1. 18th century prospect of Crosby**

The Crosby of 1716 had already been in existence — if the Viking roots of its place-name are accurate — for hundreds of years before this picture was painted on a pottery plaque. Great Crosby, as it was properly called, was a small Lancashire village inland from the Mersey shore and centred on the ancient chapel of St. Michael. This west prospect shows sailing ships on the river. Horsemen and pedestrians are on the shore — a well-used north/south route in those days of hazardous roads. Behind are the sand-dunes (with rabbits) and, on the right, a small house for the keeper of the warren — for rabbits were an important part of the local economy. Beyond can be seen cattle grazing on the open pasture land of Great Crosby Marsh and some fields which back on to the village itself. Not visible on this photograph, but depicted on the left horizon of the actual plaque, was Little Crosby windmill. (The original plaque was in the collection at Liverpool Museum but is missing, believed to have been destroyed in the Blitz. It can now be admired only at second-hand through drawings and paintings).

CHURCH. GREAT CROSBY.

## 2. St. Michael's old church

Known as Crosby Chapel, St. Michael's was a chapel-of-ease in the mother parish of Sefton. It was situated in the Church Road area (now a car park), opposite the present-day St. Helen's Roman Catholic Church and 'Sandalwood' residences. The date of the original foundation is not known; however it was mentioned in documents as far back as the 15th century and was dedicated to St. Michael *in Monte Tumba,* a pre-Reformation variant dedication, feast day 16th October. (The Crosby goose-feast, also in mid-October, was a time of festivities for the whole community). When the old chapel fell into disrepair it was rebuilt (after 1769); as can be seen in this drawing, the new chapel had a square brick tower. This chapel was demolished in 1864; the tower in 1880.

## 3. St. Michael's Well

Great Crosby's holy site - a well dedicated to St. Michael - has long been commemorated by a simple cross. This has been relocated and renovated several times but still remains in the vicinity of Crosby Chapel. In this photograph, houses by The Green and the awnings of shops on Liverpool Road frame the monument.

The Old Mill, Gt. Crosby.

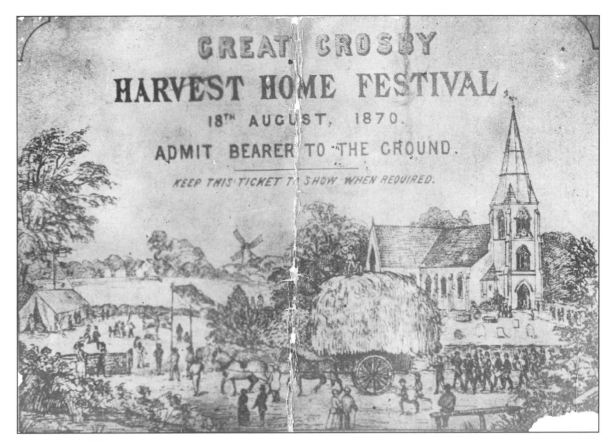

**4. Harvest Home**

This ticket for the Harvest Home Festival, 18th August 1870, helps to illustrate Crosby's relatively recent rural past. Pictured is St. Luke's parish church, built in 1854 about a quarter of a mile from the old Crosby Chapel. (St. Luke's Day - 18th October - retains the seasonal link with the village's traditional festival). In the foreground a cart is laden with grain crops on its way, perhaps, to Great Crosby Mill - which can be seen in the distance.

**5. Crosby Mill, Moor Lane**

The cap (or tower) windmill on Moor Lane was built by lord of the manor William Joseph Blundell in 1813/14. It replaced the mill in Little Crosby - a village which had, until then, an unbroken milling tradition dating back to the 13th century. In contrast, Great Crosby's two medieval windmills had long since disappeared. Crosby's windmills - together with the school founded by merchant tailor John Harrison in 1620 - would have been landmarks on the shore for sailors: certainly they were depicted on navigation charts. (A mill was on the 1716 plaque, as must have been the school-house). The Moor Lane mill was powered successively by wind, steam, gas and electricity until it ceased activity in 1972. It eventually became a private residence.

**6. Crosby Village**

This view of Great Crosby village, looking along Liverpool Road, dates from the early years of the twentieth century - electric trams are running and the poles supporting the cables can be clearly seen. In the distance are the distinctive black-and-white mock-Tudor buildings, constructed in 1901, which still stand at the junction with Moor Lane.

### 7.8.9. Crosby Village

The view (above) of Liverpool Road looks in the opposite direction to photograph 6. Crosby Police Station can be seen in the distance: the Police Station was situated at the junction of Liverpool Road, Little Crosby Lane (later Road) and Pinfold Lane (later Cooks Road). The original building was extended in 1892/3 to cover the site of the village pinfold (where stray farm animals had hitherto been kept). It was superseded by the Police Station in Waterloo which opened in 1978. On the left of the picture, drapers M. M. & E. Christian are advertising millinery and maids' caps.

The fine photo (above right) dates from the late 1920s. It shows the expanse of Liverpool Road from the George Hotel (built in the early 19th century) to the Dining Rooms and Supper Bar. The tramlines on this cobbled street have been taken up and filled in.

Another view of Liverpool Road (below right) shows shops on the site of what became Moor Lane bypass. The bypass was proposed as early as 1930 but was not constructed until the 1950s.

## 10. SS. Peter & Paul R.C. Church

Further along Liverpool Road, adjacent to the site of one of Great Crosby's medieval windmills, is the Roman Catholic Church of SS. Peter & Paul. This photo shows the original building which dated from 1826, only one year after the inauguration of the mission in Great Crosby. Depicted in stained glass in the fine east window were the seven Sacraments of the Roman Catholic Church. This building was demolished in 1894 to make way for the present church.

## 11. Boulder Stone

Great Crosby's most ancient relic - the Boulder Stone - was also a feature of Liverpool Road. This 20-ton mass of gypsum - an 'erratic' boulder, believed to have been carried south from Cumberland by some Ice Age glacier - was unearthed from a depth of 20 feet in Cooks Lane (now Manor Road) in 1898. It was set up at the junction of Liverpool Road and Islington, opposite the site of Crown Buildings (which were erected six years later). This view looks along Liverpool Road from the village and also shows, on the right, some of the Islington shops. Jack Johnson - the elderly gentleman in the foreground - can be seen again in photograph 43.

### 12. Boulder Stone

In October 1926 the Boulder Stone was moved from Great Crosby village to the Recreation Ground, Coronation Road. The move took three days to complete - cracks appeared in the erratic, so great care had to be taken. On the left is M. & E. Cook, glass & hardware store - now the route of the Moor Lane bypass. In the background to all the activity can be seen Liverpool Road Methodist Church, mute reminder of Great Crosby's original ornate Wesleyan edifice (erected 1863, demolished 1890) whose bricks were 're-cycled' to build the Mersey Road Methodist Church, Blundellsands. Some Great Crosby residents objected to this; they renovated and enlarged the former Sunday School, thus maintaining a Methodist presence in the village.

## 13. Great Crosby Urban District Council
Great Crosby had been governed by a Local Board of Health since 1863. In 1894 the Board, with its limited powers, was superseded by an Urban District Council. Alexandra Hall, which had opened on 14th November 1888, functioned as the local council's offices and meeting room as well as public Assembly Rooms for social occasions. This photograph shows the Council Chairman's ornate raised seat; inkwells and pens are on the table.

## 14. Great Crosby Carnegie Library
One of Great Crosby Urban District's first civic schemes was a free public library. This was completed in 1905 with financial assistance from the Scottish-American philanthropist Andrew Carnegie. The site was in College Road (formerly Marsh Lane), some distance from the village centre, but adjacent to Alexandra Hall. This early photo shows the library in almost glorious isolation.

## 15. Great Crosby Fire Brigade

The men of the Crosby Fire Brigade are pictured outside Alexandra Hall waiting to enter the Crosby Carnival procession in about 1907. The canopy over the entrance doorway is no more; in the stained glass were depicted Great Crosby's civic badge - a cross - and the words 'Alexandra Hall'. This brigade was founded in 1894 but had been preceded by the Crosby and Blundellsands Volunteer Brigade. For many years the fire engine was kept in College Road (Great Crosby's 'civic' centre) - but the stables and fire bell were in the old village. The men therefore had to run with the horses and link up with the fire engine before they could set out to tackle a fire!

## 16. Crosby Carnival 1913

The Crosby Carnival was a major social event in the year. This photograph, taken in Coronation Road looking up towards the village, shows the nine vehicles entered by Edward Armstrong, coal merchant and furniture remover, in the 1913 Carnival.

**17. Thorpes Lane**

Coronation Road was earlier known as Thorpes Lane; it was re-named to commemorate the coronation of King Edward VII in 1902. This photograph shows a single-storey thatched cottage and a two-storey house, plus some local residents, in the old - muddy - country lane.

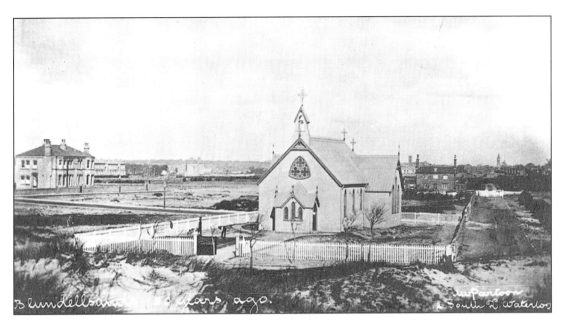

Blundellsands 50 years ago. W.Parton South R. Waterloo.

## 18. St. Nicholas's Church

Rural Crosby, both inland and near the shore, gradually developed during the l9th century. St. Nicholas's Church ministered originally to Anglicans in the community of Brighton-le-Sands, and had developed from the earlier school and licensed chapel of St. Barnabas. The iron church, pictured here about 1870 with sandhills at the gate, was situated near the modern junction of Warren Road and Agnes Road. The permanent church was built between 1873/4 and was known as St. Nicholas, Blundellsands. Mersey Road, on the right, leads to the level crossing over the railway; by the crossing is the original Crosby Station.

## 19. Crosby & Blundellsands Station

The railway had come to the area in 1848 with the construction of the Waterloo to Southport line; later the track was extended to Liverpool. The line hugged the coast, avoiding the original village, but passing over Great Crosby Marsh - later developed as Blundellsands. This view of the Crosby and Blundellsands Station, taken from Agnes Road, must be dated after 1881 when the station was moved from its original site. A horse-drawn carriage appears to be awaiting a passenger outside the station.

**20. Brooke Road Level Crossing**
Unlike Mersey Road, Brooke Road (formerly Brighton Road) retained its level crossing. This view, looking west, shows the gates which were opened by the crossing keeper. A two-seater horse-drawn buggy can be seen; and a milk cart (or milk 'dandy') is being pushed along, perhaps by the milkman. In the distance is the 'Brooke Hotel'.

**21. Brooke Hotel**
This fine photograph of the 'Brooke Hotel' dates from before its 1922 reconstruction. Barrels of beer are being delivered by a dray pulled by two horses. The proprietor of the beer house, George Clarke, is perhaps in the picture; certainly many local residents posed for the photographer. On the right, hens can be seen pecking in the mud.

ROYAL HOTEL, WATERLOO.   W.42.

## 22. Royal Hotel, Waterloo

The grand hostelry now known as the 'Royal Hotel' was originally planned as the 'Crosby Seabank Hotel' for visitors intent on taking advantage of the area's clear waters and golden sands. Its opening in 1816 coincided with the first anniversary of the famous battle: 'Waterloo' was by then a household name, and at a grand dinner the 'Royal Waterloo Hotel' at Crosby Seabank was inaugurated. Subsequently the community itself also became known as Waterloo - a fashionable sea-bathing resort and expanding residential area - and the name Crosby Seabank gradually fell into disuse.

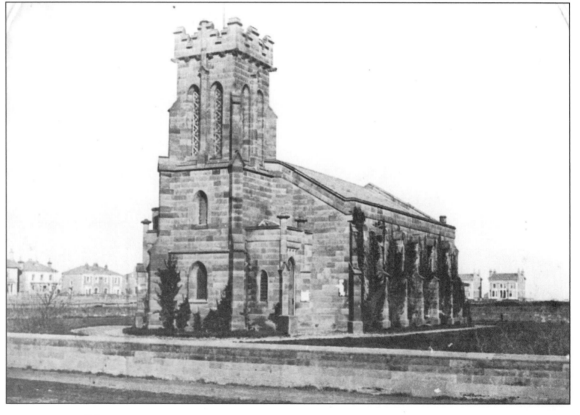

## 23. Christ Church

This photograph of Christ Church shows the original building which was opened in 1840 to serve Anglicans in the Waterloo community. The southern part of Waterloo was, administratively, part of the ancient Litherland township; but in 1856 it was combined with its fast-growing neighbour on the Mersey shore to form the new Waterloo-with-Seaforth Local Board of Health. Christ Church was enlarged twice before being demolished at the end of the nineteenth century to make way for a new, spacious church.

## 24. Liver Hotel

The building now known as the 'Liver Hotel' also dates from the early years of the Waterloo community, though identification as an inn came only towards the middle of the 19th century. This photograph shows the hostelry before its surrounding wall was built; and as no tramlines can be seen, this would suggest a date prior to 1899. The road surface appears to be undergoing repair with the aid of a steam roller - and perhaps the barrel contains water for the job in hand?

## 25. Crosby Road North

This long view of the 'Liver' shows a cobbled road with tramlines and two trams about to pass. Close inspection reveals a coach and horses outside the hotel.

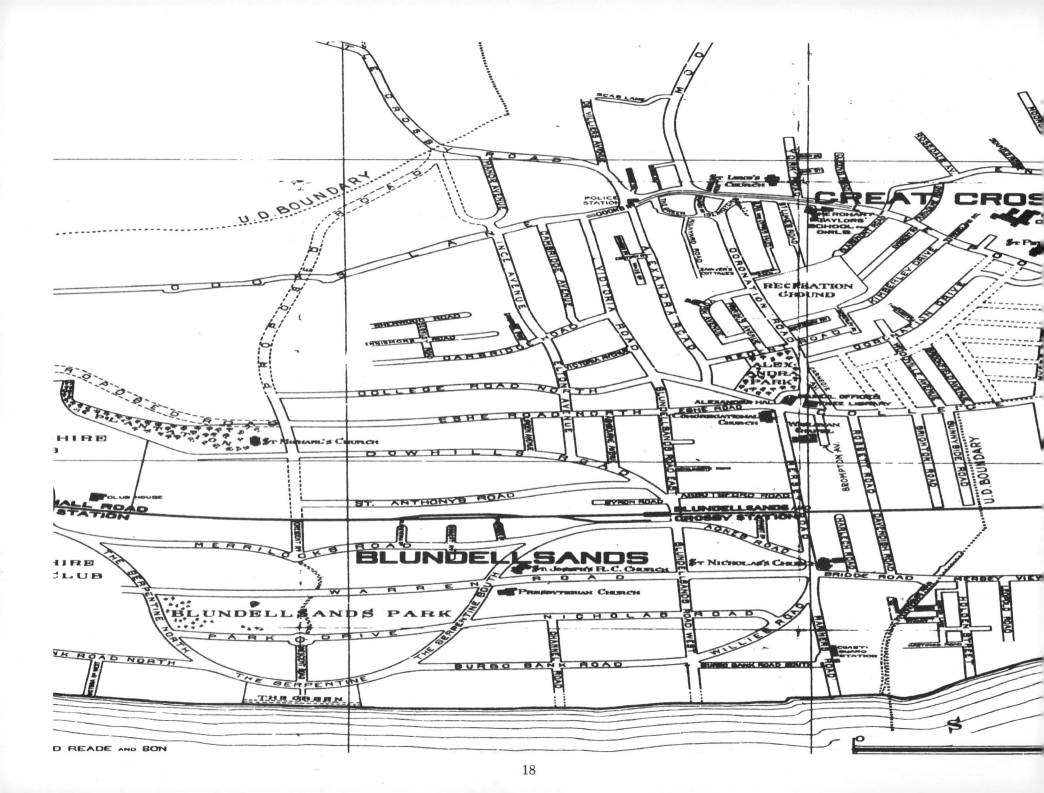

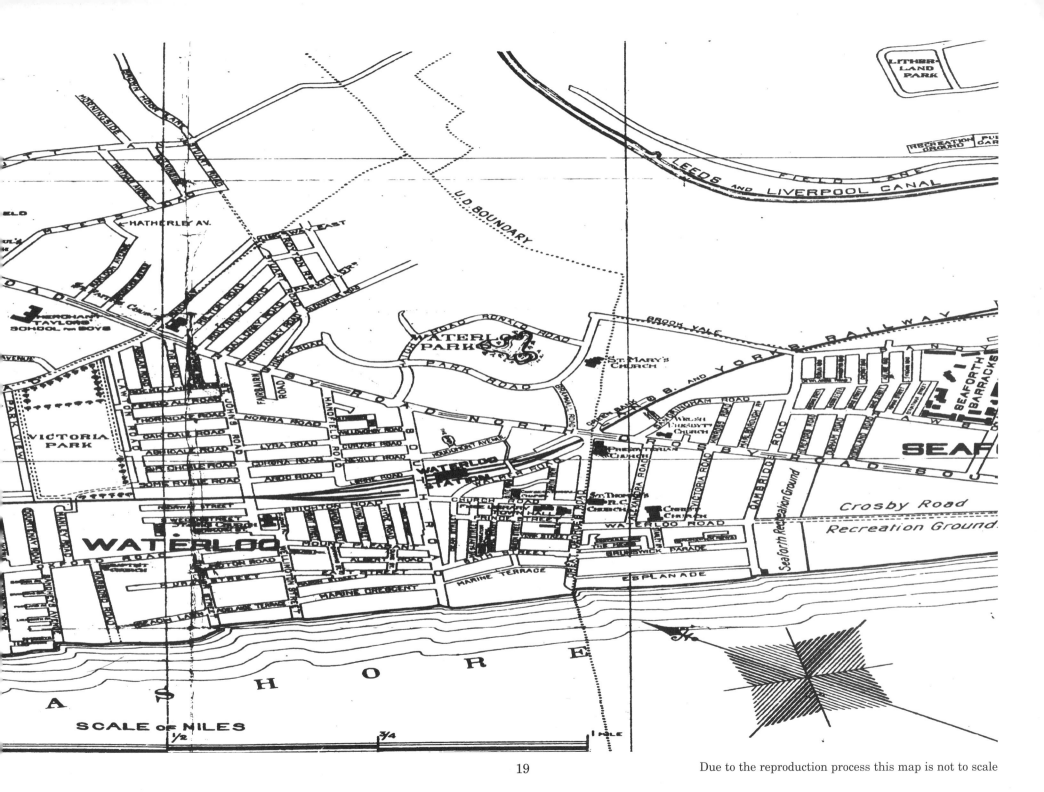

LITHER-
LAND
PARK

RECREATION
GROUND

LEEDS AND LIVERPOOL CANAL

FIELD LANE

U.D. BOUNDARY

BROOK VALE

MORNINGSIDE

HUDSON ROAD

HATHERLEY AV.

MERCHANT
TAYLORS
SCHOOL for BOYS

RAILWAY EAST

WATERLOO
PARK

St. MARY'S
CHURCH

SEAFORTH
BARRACKS

VICTORIA
PARK

HORNDALE ROAD

OAK DALE ROAD

NORMA ROAD

LYRA ROAD

CORONA ROAD

ARDO ROAD

RONALD ROAD

PARK ROAD

BRAMHALL ROAD

PARK ROAD NORTH

WELSH
PRESBYT.
CHURCH

BIRKINGHAM ROAD

SEAF

Crosby Road
Recreation Ground

PRESBYTERIAN
CHURCH

WATERLOO
STATION

VICTORIA ROAD

WATERLOO ROAD

St. THOMAS
R.C.
CHURCH

CHURCH ROAD

LIBRARY
TOWN HALL
PRINCE STREET

CHRIST
CHURCH

Seaforth Recreation Ground

OXAM BRIDGE ROAD

WATERLOO

MARINE CRESCENT

MARINE TERRACE

ESPLANADE

SHORE

SCALE of MILES

1/2          3/4          1 MILE

19                                    Due to the reproduction process this map is not to scale

**26. South Road**

This photograph of South Road - Waterloo's thriving shopping thoroughfare - looks towards Crosby Road from the station. The street lights are sited down the centre of the road and the actual lamps are halfway up each column. Outside the shops can be seen many handcarts, perhaps waiting to be filled with ordered goods and then pulled by delivery boys to local houses.

### 27. South Road

Another photograph of South Road, this one takes a view from the corner of Mount Pleasant. The occasion was a civic procession on 17th June 1916 during Roll of Honour Week. This was one of the many fundraising events held in Waterloo during the First World War. The proceeds were to benefit soldiers' dependents and also disabled ex-servicemen. The parade wound its way from Seaforth Sands Station (Overhead Railway) through Waterloo to the Town Hall in Great George's Road.

### 28. Mount Pleasant

Waterloo Post Office was at the junction of Mount Pleasant and South Road. Posing in the road between the Post Office and the general store are some local workmen and shoppers and - perhaps - a postman. The photograph is undated, but probably taken before the First World War.

21

**29. St. John's Road**
St. John's Road, Waterloo, still has its level crossing. This photograph shows boys pulling a handcart over the crossing. The hoarding on the left advertises Threlfall's Blue Label Beer; while the Lancashire & Yorkshire Railway Company's notice on the gate reads "Children must not lean upon the gates".

### 30.31. Waterloo train disaster

Waterloo was the scene of a serious railway accident in 1903. On Wednesday 15th July, at 4.30 pm, a train from Liverpool rounded the bend in the Five Lamps Tunnel at too high a speed. The engine left the rails, collided with the footbridge by Waterloo Station and crashed on to the platform. Six people died in the accident and many were injured.

The photograph (left) shows the engine which, through the force of the crash, ended up facing southwards. Another view (below) shows the carriages and onlookers.

**32. Waterloo-with-Seaforth Urban District Council**
The Waterloo-with-Seaforth Urban District Council, with its wide local responsibilities, superseded the old Local Board of Health in 1895. The photograph shows members and officials of the U.D.C. on an outing to view the Hoylake Promenade Scheme on 10th June 1899.

### 33.34. Marine Gardens

Plans for developing the Waterloo seafront must have occupied the mind of the local authority for many years. The portion originally known as Marine Terrace Green was developed from 1931; the photograph (left) shows landscaping underway. The project was aided by grants to support work-schemes for the unemployed. Shown subsequently in all their glory (below), the new seafront gardens and promenade were opened in 1932.

NEW MARINE GARDENS, WATERLOO.

**35. Waterloo Library**

This free public library in Church Road - symbol of Waterloo-with-Seaforth's civic pride - was another 'Carnegie' institution. It was opened in 1908 by Lord Derby and was modelled on William Gladstone's private library at Hawarden. It was destroyed by an incendiary bomb on 3rd May 1941.

**36. Church Road**

Taken looking northwards this photograph of Church Road shows, on the left, one of the statues which stood outside the library. Beyond that is the Waterloo Public Museum, then the Police Station. On the right, at the corner of Olive Road, is the Waterloo Congregational Church.

**37. Waterloo-with-Seaforth Fire Brigade**

This splendid photograph, taken about 1895, shows the Waterloo-with-Seaforth Fire Brigade and some local councillors. They are portrayed with the fire engine (though without the horses) and a hose cart. An assortment of equipment, including ladders, handaxes and coils of rope, can also be seen. Waterloo's fire station was in Prince Street.

### 38.39.40. Wrecks

Waterloo and Crosby's coastal location has meant that, over the years, the communities have seen many ships wrecked on the shore. The 'Matador' (above left) was a Russian barque out of Riga, wrecked off Mariner's Road on 16th October 1902. The crew were rescued by the West Kirby and Hoylake lifeboat.

A coal ship, the 'Heraclides' (above) ran aground in 1902. A fleet of carts had to be used to ferry the cargo from the beach to waiting transport.

One of the best-known local wrecks was the schooner 'Lily Baynes' (below left) which grounded on the shore at Blundellsands in November 1907 during a violent storm. The captain and three crew members clung to the rigging throughout the night before wading ashore at low water the next morning. The wreck, still with its cargo of timber aboard, attracted large crowds of sightseers.

**41.42. Coast Erosion**
The shore has also proved treacherous for local residents. The mouth of the River Alt migrated up and down the Crosby foreshore causing, in the process, both erosion and accretion on the coast. The erosion has, in some cases, resulted in whole houses tumbling into the sea. These two photographs, dating from 1930, show the results of erosion at The Serpentine, Blundellsands - a road which, when built in 1888, was over 70 yards from the sea. Subsequent sea-defence works have constrained the wandering Alt.

**43. Jack Johnson**

Oblivious to possible danger, however, a few people (such as Jack Johnson) chose to live <u>on</u> the shore. The official address of this local 'character' was Alt Cottage, Hall Road: the ramshackle residence dug into the sand was his home for nearly fifty years from about 1871. Nicknamed 'Roast Beef' (because of his ruddy complexion) or 'The Hermit of the Sandhills', Johnson made a living from a variety of shore-side activities including cockling and beachcombing: a creel for cockles can be seen strapped to his back. In spite of appearances, Johnson was said to be noted for his cleanliness.

Mr Melly On Waterloo Shore

### 44.45. Henry Melly, aviator

Another unusual use for the shore was as an airfield. Henry Melly was a pioneer aviator who was renowned internationally as well as being a local celebrity. He studied aviation in France in 1910; then founded the Liverpool Aviation Flying School in Sandheys Avenue, Waterloo. Pictured below are two of his machines, including a 50 h.p. Gnome-Bleriot, in 1911. In July of that year Melly made a record-breaking flight from Waterloo to Manchester: 40 minutes.

## 46. Horsedrawn bus

A slower means of transport was the omnibus - this one, for example, was drawn by four horses. It was photographed at election time in the late 19th century outside Park House, Waterloo: the posters read "Blackburn & Cross the farmers' friends" and "Peace and plenty". The driver wears protection against bad weather.

## 47. Horsedrawn bus

This photograph was taken at Five Lamps, Waterloo - then a traffic island complete with post box, later a war memorial. A two-horse bus is the main feature; but also in view is a poster advertising 'Technical Classes: Lectures' and, on the right, a milk 'dandy'. The house behind the bus is on the site of the present-day fire and ambulance stations.

**48. Horsedrawn bus**
Dating from the late 19th century, this fine picture shows a two-horse bus at the Great Crosby village terminus. The passengers who are alighting at the 'George Hotel' include a woman wearing a boater and carrying a parasol. In the background is Callis's workshop ('whitesmith and blacksmith'), since replaced by mock-Tudor buildings. The 'George Hotel' was demolished and rebuilt on the same site (though on a new building line to allow for road-widening) in 1929.

**49. Electric tram**

In 1899 the Liverpool Overhead Railway Company commenced a 2½ mile electric tram service from Seaforth Sands Station to Great Crosby. This photograph, taken in Crosby Road about 1902, shows an original double-decker with an open top and an exposed platform for the driver. The high side rails were to protect upper-deck passengers from being harmed by the trolley-rope of a passing tramcar.

34

**50. Crosby Charter celebrations 1937**

1937 was a notable date in the history of the Crosby area. In that year, the Urban Districts of Great Crosby (which included Little Crosby) and Waterloo-with-Seaforth combined to form the Borough of Crosby. Lord Derby presented the Royal Charter to the town on 20th July - and thus triggered a wide variety of celebratory events. The photograph shows one of the more solemn occasions - the Charter Sunday procession to lay a wreath at the Five Lamps war memorial. Pictured in Waterloo Road, 'en route' from morning service at Christ Church, is the Charter Mayor, Alderman H. T. Hancock, flanked by the Chaplain and Town Clerk, and followed by local dignitaries. The ancient villages and the younger communities were now united - ready to face the future together.

# FURTHER READING

Although by no means comprehensive, this is a fair selection of material relating to the topics covered in the book and to the pre-war history of the Crosby area in general. All items listed are available for consultation in the Local History Department at Crosby Library. Readers may wish to pursue particular lines of enquiry beyond the limitations of this list: Sefton's Local History librarians would be pleased to advise.

| | |
|---|---|
| BAINES, E. | History of the County Palatine & Duchy of Lancaster. 2 vols. (1868/70) |
| BAINES, E. | History, directory and gazetteer of the County Palatine of Lancaster. (1825) |
| BLUNDELL, N. | The great diurnal of Nicholas Blundell (edited by Frank Tyrer) Vol. 1 1702-1711 (1968) Vol. 2 1712-1719 (1970) Vol. 3 1720-1728 (1972) |
| BLUNDELL, W. | Cavalier: letters of William Blundell 1620-98. (1933) |
| BOOTLE TIMES | 1881 to date (microfilm) |
| CROSBY HERALD | 1895 to date (microfilm) |
| DIRECTORIES of Waterloo, Blundellsands, Crosby & Seaforth (various dates) | |
| FARRER, W. | The Victoria History of the County of Lancashire 8 vols. (1911) |
| GELL, R. | Illustrated survey of railway stations between Southport & Liverpool 1848-1986. (1986) |
| GREGSON, M. | Portfolio of fragments relative to the history & antiquities of the County Palatine of Lancaster 3rd ed. (1869) |
| HULL, R. C. | Social differentiation in a North Liverpool suburb: the case of Great Crosby & Waterloo 1841-1901. (thesis) (1989) |
| LAMB, C. | Story of Crosby. (1936) |
| LEWIS, J. R. | Birth of Waterloo in notes & sketches. (1982) |
| LUFT, H. M. | A History of Merchant Taylors' School, Crosby, 1620-1970 (1970) |
| MANNEX, P. | History, topography and directory of mid-Lancashire. (1854) |
| MAYER, J. | On Liverpool pottery (in Transactions of the Historic Society of Lancashire and Cheshire, Vol. 7, 1855) |
| SEFTON MBC, Libraries | Crosby in the past: a photographic record of the history of Crosby & district (1977) |
| SEFTON MBC, Planning | Notes on Waterloo. (1989) |
| TYRER, F. | Crosby and district in English history. |
| TYRER, F. | The Windmills of Crosby. (1972) |
| WHALE, D. | Lost villages of Liverpool. 3 vols. (1984) |
| WILLIAMS, T. | Halmote court rolls of the manor of Great Crosby 1452-1885. (1956) |
| WILLIAMS, T. | Probate records of Crosby & district 1466-1825. (1973) |
| WILLIAMS, T. | Thornton in Sefton parish (1947) |

# GUIDE TO THE ILLUSTRATIONS

Where possible, the library's catalogue number is given; some photographs are, however, as yet uncatalogued. The code "LS" indicates a print taken from a lantern slide. For further information contact the Local History Department at Crosby Library, Crosby Road North, Waterloo, Liverpool L22 0LQ. Tel: 0151-928 6487/8.